MEXICAN REVOLUTION

THE FIGHT FOR FREEDOM THAT SHAPED MODERN MEXICO (1910-1920)

DANIEL WRINN

CONTENTS

GET YOUR FREE COPY OF WW2: SPIES, SNIPERS AND THE WORLD AT WAR

Enter into a World of Warfare History

Explore Military History And Warfare Stories From The 20th Century

Get your free copy of WW2: Spies, Snipers, and Tales of the World at War and dive into the stories that changed the world.

Send me my free Ebook

Never miss a new release by signing up for my free readers group. You'll also get WW2: Spies, Snipers and Tales of the World at War delivered to your inbox. (You can unsubscribe at any time.) Go to wrinnmilitaryhistory.com to join.

INTRODUCTION

"Mátalos en caliente" *(Kill them on the spot)*

— PORFIRIO DÍAZ

THE MEXICAN REVOLUTION TOOK PLACE BETWEEN 1910 and 1920. It was a period of intense conflict, social upheaval, and political change. This decade-long struggle resulted in the overthrow of Porfirio Díaz, whose authoritarian regime had controlled Mexico for over thirty-five years. The revolution reshaped the country's political landscape, introducing new ideologies and reforms that would shape Mexico for decades to come. While often romanticized as a fight for justice and equality, the revolution was far from a unified movement. It was a complex and often brutal civil war involving multiple factions, each with its own vision of Mexico's future. The conflict's legacy is not simply one of liberation but also of profound political reorganization and the emergence of a new elite.

The Mexican Revolution was not only about overthrowing Díaz; it was also about addressing deep-seated social and economic inequalities that had plagued the country for centuries. Land ownership, labor rights, and political representation were key issues at the heart of the revolution. Rural peasants, laborers, and indigenous communities demanded access to land and fair treatment, while intellectuals and political reformers sought democratic governance and political inclusion. Despite the promises made by revolutionary leaders, the reality of the conflict was far more complex, and the path to meaningful reform was riddled with setbacks and compromises.

At its core, the Mexican Revolution was a reaction to the rigid social structure and the concentration of wealth and power in the hands of a few. While some of its leaders, like Francisco Madero, envisioned a liberal democracy, others, such as Emiliano Zapata and Pancho Villa, sought more radical social reforms, including land redistribution and the rights of the peasantry. The revolution ultimately led to significant changes, including the drafting of the 1917 Constitution, which remains in force today. However, the path to these reforms was fraught with violence, betrayal, and shifting alliances.

By the early twentieth century, Mexico was a deeply divided society. Under the rule of Porfirio Díaz, the country had experienced a period of modernization and economic growth, but this prosperity came at a cost. Much of the economic development that occurred during Díaz's regime was driven by foreign investment, particularly from the United States and Europe, which benefitted the wealthy elite and foreign capitalists while leaving the majority of Mexicans in poverty.

Porfirio Díaz's leadership, often referred to as *El*

Porfiriato, was marked by authoritarianism and cronyism. Although Díaz is credited with bringing stability to Mexico following decades of civil unrest, his regime maintained control through a combination of political repression, rigged elections, and manipulation of local power structures. His government was supported by a small but powerful oligarchy of landowners, military officials, and industrialists. This elite class controlled vast swathes of land and resources, while the peasantry, which made up the majority of the population, toiled in conditions of near-feudal servitude on large estates known as haciendas.

The Díaz regime's policies favored the expansion of large agricultural and industrial enterprises, often at the expense of small landowners and indigenous communities. Land reform was one of the most pressing issues of the time, as millions of rural Mexicans were dispossessed of their land, forced to work on haciendas or migrate to cities in search of work. This concentration of land ownership and the exploitation of labor were key factors in the growing discontent that eventually led to revolution.

Another important factor was political disenfranchisement. Díaz's government maintained a facade of democracy by holding periodic elections, but these were little more than formalities, with Díaz and his allies manipulating the results to ensure their continued dominance. Opposition parties and independent political movements were suppressed, and political dissidents were frequently imprisoned or exiled. This stifling political climate led to growing frustration among Mexico's intellectual and middle classes, who sought democratic reforms and greater political participation.

The first significant challenge to Díaz's rule came from Francisco Madero, a wealthy landowner and political reformer who advocated for free elections and an end to Díaz's dictatorship. Madero's ideas gained traction among the middle class, who were frustrated with the lack of political representation, and among the rural poor, who hoped for land reform. In 1910, Madero ran for president against Díaz, but the election was rigged, and Díaz declared himself the winner. This fraudulent election became the catalyst for the revolution.

The social and economic inequalities, combined with the lack of political freedom, created the perfect storm for revolution. It was not simply a rebellion of the poor against the rich but a multi-faceted conflict involving different regions, classes, and ideologies. Some factions, like those led by Emiliano Zapata, focused on land redistribution and the rights of indigenous communities. Others, like Pancho Villa, sought to challenge the centralized power in Mexico City and promote regional autonomy.

The revolution also attracted foreign interest, particularly from the United States, which had significant economic interests in Mexico. American corporations owned a large portion of Mexico's land and resources, particularly in the mining and oil sectors. As the revolution progressed, the U.S. government became increasingly involved, sometimes supporting different factions in the conflict in order to protect American interests. This foreign involvement added another layer of complexity to the revolution, as various factions sought to either gain or resist American support.

Through a balanced examination of the revolution's causes and outcomes, we will avoid romanticizing the conflict or portraying it as a simple struggle between good and evil. The Mexican Revolution was a multifaceted conflict that involved competing interests and ideologies. While it resulted in significant reforms, it also led to immense suffering and a new political order that, in many ways, continued to reflect the hierarchical power structures it sought to dismantle.

PORFIRIO DÍAZ'S RULE

"So far from God, so close to the United States."

— *PORFIRIO DÍAZ*

PORFIRIO DÍAZ'S RISE TO POWER IN MEXICO WAS ONE of both military prowess and political cunning. Born in 1830 in Oaxaca, Díaz was a mestizo of modest origins who built his reputation as a skilled military leader during Mexico's wars with the United States and later in the fight against the French during the Second Mexican Empire. After the fall of Emperor Maximilian in 1867, Díaz aligned himself with the liberal forces of Benito Juárez, though he would later become disillusioned with Juárez's continued hold on power.

In 1876, Díaz first came to power through a military coup, seizing control from President Sebastián Lerdo de Tejada under the banner of the Plan de Tuxtepec, which called for no re-election, among other liberal reforms. Ironically, once Díaz consolidated power, he amended this principle, extending his own rule for more than three decades, a period known as El Porfiriato. From 1876 to 1911—with the exception of a brief interlude from 1880 to 1884—Díaz ruled Mexico with an iron grip, using a combination of political repression, manipulation, and selective modernization to maintain control.

Economically, Díaz's policies were focused on development and industrialization. He opened the country to foreign investment, particularly from the United States, Britain, and France, and encouraged infrastructure projects such as the expansion of railroads and telegraphs. Mexico's economy grew rapidly under his leadership, but the benefits were unevenly distributed. The elites, many of them large landowners and industrialists, prospered, while the majority of the population— rural peasants and urban laborers—remained in poverty.

One of Díaz's main strategies to maintain power was to align himself with foreign interests. He sold off vast amounts of land to foreign investors, particularly in the mining, oil, and agricultural sectors. This made Mexico dependent on foreign capital and allowed Díaz to solidify his relationship with the wealthy elite, who supported his regime in return for favorable policies. However, this strategy also meant that Mexico's economic sovereignty was compromised, and its wealth was concentrated in the hands of a few.

Politically, Díaz used a combination of patronage and force to control the country. He ruled through a network of loyal *caciques* (local political bosses) who helped maintain order in the provinces. Opposition parties were allowed to exist but had no real power, and elections were often rigged to ensure that Díaz or his allies remained in control. Dissenters were dealt with harshly. Political opponents were often exiled, imprisoned, or silenced through intimidation.

Díaz's authoritarian approach brought a superficial sense of stability and order to Mexico. His regime successfully suppressed uprisings and rebellions that had plagued the country throughout the nineteenth century. However, beneath the surface, resentment simmered among the population. The prosperity brought by foreign investment and industrialization was uneven, and the poor were becoming increasingly frustrated with their lack of opportunities.

One of the most glaring problems during the Porfiriato was the deep social and economic inequality that existed throughout the country. The benefits of Díaz's policies were felt primarily by the wealthy elite, who lived in the cities and owned vast estates in the countryside. For the rural peasantry and the working class, life under Díaz was harsh and unforgiving. Land ownership was a particularly contentious issue, as a small number of families owned the majority of the land, while millions of Mexicans worked as *peones* (peasant laborers) on haciendas.

The hacienda system was essentially a form of feudalism, in which landowners had near-complete control over the lives of the peasants who worked for them. The peones were often paid in *vales*, a form of credit that could only be used at stores owned by the landowner, creating a cycle of debt and dependency that made it nearly impossible for workers to escape their conditions. This system allowed the wealthy landowners to accumulate even more land and wealth, while the peasants remained impoverished.

In addition to the rural population, the urban working class also faced difficult conditions. The rapid industrialization promoted by Díaz created a demand for labor in Mexico's growing cities, but wages were low, and working conditions were often dangerous. Labor laws were minimal, and workers had little recourse if they were injured on the job or mistreated by their employers. Strikes and labor unrest were common, but they were typically met with brutal repression by the government, which sided with the business owners and foreign investors who had helped finance Díaz's modernization projects.

As the gap between the rich and the poor grew wider, discontent began to spread across the country. The concentration of land and wealth in the hands of a small elite, coupled with the lack of political representation for the majority of the population, created a fertile ground for rebellion. The rural peasants were becoming increasingly frustrated with their lack of access to land and the oppressive conditions under which they lived and worked. In the cities, laborers and intellectuals began to question the legitimacy of Díaz's rule and called for political and social reforms.

While Díaz's regime was able to suppress these discontented groups for many years, by the early twentieth century, cracks were beginning to appear in the system. The long-standing grievances of the rural and urban poor, combined with the lack of political freedom, created an environment ripe for revolution. Díaz's authoritarian rule, once seen as a stabilizing force, was now viewed as the root cause of Mexico's social and economic problems.

By 1910, opposition to Díaz's rule was gaining

momentum. One of the most prominent figures to emerge during this period was Francisco Madero, a wealthy landowner from the state of Coahuila who had become increasingly critical of Díaz's dictatorship. Unlike many of the other opposition figures of the time, Madero was not a radical revolutionary but a liberal reformer who believed in democratic principles and sought to bring about change through peaceful means.

Madero's opposition to Díaz began to crystallize in 1908 when Díaz gave an interview to an American journalist in which he stated that Mexico was ready for democracy and that he would welcome an opposition party in the upcoming elections. Taking Díaz at his word, Madero wrote a political manifesto titled *La Sucesión Presidencial* (The Presidential Succession) in 1910, in which he called for free and fair elections and the end of Díaz's rule. Madero's platform was centered on political reform, specifically the establishment of democratic institutions, free elections, and the protection of individual rights.

Madero's calls for democratic reform struck a chord with many Mexicans, particularly those in the middle class who had become frustrated with Díaz's authoritarian rule. His message of peaceful change through democratic means resonated with those who sought political participation and an end to the cronyism that had defined the Porfiriato. Madero's candidacy for the 1910 presidential election quickly gained support, and it appeared that he might pose a serious challenge to Díaz.

However, Díaz had no intention of allowing a legitimate opposition to emerge.

THE ELECTION OF 1910

"Effective suffrage, no re-election."

— FRANCISCO MADERO

The Mexican Revolution's roots can be traced directly to the 1910 presidential election, which became a flashpoint for long-simmering discontent with the rule of Porfirio Díaz. By this time, Díaz had been in power for over thirty-five years, using a combination of force, political manipulation, and economic partnerships with foreign interests to maintain control. Although his policies had brought stability and economic growth, the benefits were largely confined to a small elite, while the majority of Mexicans—particularly peasants and laborers—remained impoverished and politically disenfranchised.

In 1908, Díaz made an unexpected and seemingly liberal statement during an interview with U.S. journalist James Creelman. Díaz's statement of democratic transition emboldened reformers and critics of his regime, many of whom had long feared open opposition due to the harsh repressive measures Díaz had employed throughout his rule.

Among those inspired by Díaz's declaration was Francisco Madero. Thirty-four years old at the time, Madero was a wealthy landowner from Coahuila with a strong belief in democratic principles. Madero came from a prominent family and had been educated abroad, which gave him a more cosmopolitan perspective than many of his contemporaries. Unlike more radical figures, Madero did not initially seek revolutionary upheaval. Instead, he wanted to see Mexico transformed into a democracy with free elections, a fair judicial system, and more equitable governance. His call for change was based on liberal principles rather than socialist or anarchist ideals.

In 1910, Madero launched his campaign for the presidency with a platform calling for the end of Díaz's dictatorship and the implementation of democratic reforms. His candidacy quickly gained traction, particularly among the middle class and intellectuals who were frustrated by the lack of political freedoms. However, Madero's platform also appealed to the rural poor, who hoped that democratic reforms would bring about land redistribution and greater economic opportunities. Madero presented himself as a moderate reformer, someone who could bridge the gap between the disaffected working class and the elite.

Díaz initially appeared to tolerate Madero's candidacy, perhaps viewing him as a political novice with little real power. However, as Madero's popularity grew, Díaz became increasingly alarmed. Despite his earlier statements about supporting free elections, Díaz had no intention of relinquishing power. As the election drew closer, he moved decisively to quash Madero's campaign. In June 1910, just before the election, Madero was arrested and imprisoned on charges of sedition. While Madero was behind bars, Díaz declared himself the winner of the election, ensuring his continued rule through fraud and manipulation.

Madero's arrest and the blatant rigging of the election outraged many Mexicans. It was clear that Díaz had no intention of stepping aside or allowing for genuine political competition. The frustration that had been building for decades among the rural poor, laborers, and the intellectual class now had a clear focus: the overthrow of Díaz's dictatorship. Madero's imprisonment, rather than silencing opposition, galvanized the resistance movement.

Following his arrest, Madero was detained in San Luis Potosí, a city in central Mexico. However, he managed to escape prison with the help of sympathetic allies and fled to the United States, where he regrouped and prepared to take more direct action against the Díaz regime. It was during this period of exile that Madero crafted one of the most important documents of the Mexican Revolution: the Plan de San Luis Potosí.

Issued on October 5, 1910, the Plan de San Luis Potosí was a manifesto that called for the Mexican people to rise up in arms against Díaz. The plan declared the recent presidential election null and void and proclaimed Madero as the provisional president of Mexico until new elections could be held. While Madero's initial candidacy had focused primarily on political reforms, the Plan de San Luis Potosí expanded his platform to include the redistribution of land—a crucial issue for the rural poor, who had been disenfranchised by Díaz's policies of selling off land to foreign investors and wealthy elites.

The Plan de San Luis Potosí resonated deeply with Mexicans across social classes. It was not only a fight against Díaz but also a movement to address the broader social and economic inequalities that had defined Mexico for decades. For the middle and upper classes, Madero's call for democracy and free elections represented a chance to end Díaz's authoritarian rule. For the rural poor and indigenous populations, the promise of land reform offered hope that they might finally gain access to land that had been taken from them over the previous decades. Madero's manifesto became the rallying cry for revolutionaries across the country, marking the formal beginning of the Mexican Revolution. The revolution would soon spiral into a complex and bloody conflict, involving various factions with different visions for the country's future.

Madero's plan called for a coordinated rebellion to begin on November 20, 1910, a date that is now commemorated as the start of the Mexican Revolution. However, due to logistical difficulties and miscommunications, the uprising did not immediately gain momentum. Initial skirmishes between government forces and small groups of revolutionaries were inconclusive. Nevertheless, the seeds of revolution had been planted, and various factions began to coalesce around Madero's call for change.

As the revolution gathered pace, different regions of Mexico became key battlegrounds, with local leaders emerging to lead the fight against Díaz's forces. In the north, one of the most important revolutionary leaders was Pancho Villa, a former bandit turned military commander who commanded a loyal following among the rural poor. Villa's forces were known for their mobility, unconventional tactics, and ability to strike swiftly at government outposts. Villa's charisma and his ability to connect with the common people made him a key figure in the northern campaign.

In the south, Emiliano Zapata became the face of the revolutionary struggle for land reform. Zapata, who hailed from the state of Morelos, had long fought for the rights of rural peasants, many of whom had been dispossessed of their land by the expansion of large haciendas under Díaz's regime. While Madero's focus was on political reform and democracy, Zapata's primary goal was land redistribution. His slogan, *Tierra y Libertad* (Land and Liberty), became synonymous with the struggle for social justice in southern Mexico. Zapata's forces, known as the Zapatistas, were fierce fighters who believed that the revolution would be incomplete without significant changes to land ownership.

By 1911, the revolution had begun to make significant gains. One of the most pivotal moments of the early phase of the conflict was the capture of Ciudad Juárez, a key border city in the north.

In May 1911, Madero's forces, led by Villa and Pascual Orozco, launched a successful assault on the city, defeating Díaz's troops and seizing control. The fall of Ciudad Juárez was a major victory for the revolutionaries and marked a turning point in the conflict. It demonstrated that Díaz's regime was vulnerable and that the revolutionaries had the ability to effectively challenge government forces, which lacked motivation and loyalty.

Following the fall of Ciudad Juárez, Díaz realized that his position was no longer tenable. On May 25, 1911, in the Treaty of Ciudad Juárez, he resigned from the presidency then went into exile in France, marking the end of more than three decades of authoritarian rule. Madero, now seen as the leader of the revolutionary movement, assumed the presidency later that year.

However, the revolution was far from over. While Madero had succeeded in ousting Díaz, he faced significant challenges in governing a country still deeply divided by social and economic inequality. Moreover, the revolutionary leaders who had supported Madero's rise to power—Villa, Zapata, and others—soon became disillusioned with his moderate approach to reform. Madero's failure to implement significant land redistribution led to a break with Zapata, whose forces continued to fight for the rights of the rural poor. The revolution that had begun as a fight to overthrow a dictator would soon spiral into a broader civil war, as various factions vied for control of Mexico's future.

RISE OF REVOLUTIONARY FACTIONS

— *EMILIANO ZAPATA*

THE FALL OF PORFIRIO DÍAZ FROM POWER IN 1911
marked the end of an era in Mexican history, bringing
to a close his thirty-five-year reign as the country's
authoritarian leader. After Francisco Madero's forces
captured Ciudad Juárez in May 1911, it became increasingly clear that Díaz's days in power were numbered.
The military defeat at Ciudad Juárez sent shockwaves
through the regime, and with revolutionary forces
gaining momentum across the country, Díaz was left
with little choice but to negotiate his exit.

On May 25, 1911, Porfirio Díaz formally resigned as
president of Mexico, acknowledging that the revolution
had made his continued rule untenable. In his resignation speech, Díaz claimed he was stepping down for the
sake of national peace, yet this act was clearly a result of

military defeat and growing pressure from the revolutionary movement. His resignation was a significant moment, not only because it marked the fall of his long-standing dictatorship but also because it demonstrated the power of popular uprisings in challenging entrenched political elites.

Following his resignation, Díaz went into exile, ultimately settling in Paris, where he would live out the rest of his life until his death in 1915. His departure symbolized the end of the Porfiriato, a period that had been characterized by political repression, economic modernization, and the consolidation of wealth and power in the hands of a few. While Díaz's fall from power was a victory for the revolutionaries, it did not immediately bring peace or prosperity to Mexico. Instead, it marked the beginning of a new and turbulent phase of the revolution, one defined by internal divisions, power struggles, and competing visions for the country's future.

With Díaz gone, the challenge for Mexico was to establish a new political order. The revolution that had begun as a movement to oust a dictator soon fractured, as different factions within the revolutionary coalition began to pursue their own interests. The fall of Díaz had removed the common enemy that had united the revolutionaries, and now the question of how to govern Mexico—and who would benefit from the revolution—became the central issue.

After Díaz's resignation, Francisco Madero assumed the presidency on November 6, 1911, taking office with widespread popular support. Madero, however, quickly discovered that leading a revolution was far easier than governing a fractured and polarized country. His presidency was marked by internal divisions, unmet expectations, and the challenge of balancing the competing demands of various revolutionary factions.

Madero's primary goal was to establish a democratic government and enact political reforms that would provide greater representation for Mexico's middle class and intellectuals. He sought to move Mexico away from the authoritarianism of Díaz's regime and toward a more liberal and constitutional form of governance. In this sense, Madero was a moderate reformer who believed in gradual change through legal and political means. He did not want to overturn the entire social order, nor did he seek to implement radical land reforms, which many of his supporters—particularly rural peasants—had hoped for.

One of the main challenges Madero faced was his inability to deliver on the promises of land redistribution. For many of the rural poor, the revolution had been about more than just political representation; it had been about gaining access to land and breaking the grip of the large hacienda owners who controlled vast amounts of territory. Madero, however, was reluctant to implement widespread land reforms, as he feared that doing so would alienate the elite landowners and disrupt the fragile political balance he was trying to maintain.

Madero's moderate approach alienated many of the revolutionary factions that had initially supported him. Emiliano Zapata, who had been one of the key leaders in the south, became increasingly frustrated with Madero's failure to address the demands of the peasantry. In the north, Pancho Villa also grew disillusioned with Madero's leadership, particularly as Madero relied on many of the same military and political elites who had served under Díaz. These elites, fearful of losing their wealth and influence, resisted any significant changes to the country's social and economic structure.

Madero's presidency was also undermined by his inability to control the military. After taking office, he allowed many of Díaz's old generals to retain their positions of power, a decision that would later prove disastrous. One of these generals, Victoriano Huerta, would ultimately betray Madero, leading a coup that overthrew him in 1913. Madero's downfall highlighted the challenges of trying to reform a deeply unequal society through moderate and legalistic means, particularly when many of the entrenched elites had no interest in giving up their privileges.

Despite his good intentions, Madero was unable to bridge the gap between the revolutionary ideals of social justice and the practical realities of governing a nation still dominated by powerful economic and political interests. His presidency, which lasted less than two years, ended in tragedy when he was arrested and executed on the orders of Huerta, plunging Mexico back into a new phase of violent conflict.

One of the most significant consequences of Madero's moderate approach was the rise of Emiliano Zapata as a revolutionary leader in southern Mexico. Zapata had supported Madero during the initial phase of the revolution, believing that Madero would fulfill his promises to address the land issue and provide relief to the rural peasantry. However, when it became clear that Madero was not willing to implement the radical land reforms that Zapata and his followers demanded, the relationship between the two men quickly deteriorated.

Zapata was a staunch advocate for the rights of the rural poor, particularly in his home state of Morelos, where large haciendas had taken over much of the land, leaving the indigenous and peasant populations with little or no access to land for farming. For Zapata, the revolution was not just about political change; it was about economic justice and the redistribution of land. When Madero failed to act on this issue, Zapata broke with him and issued his own revolutionary manifesto, known as the Plan de Ayala, in November 1911.

The Plan de Ayala was a radical document that called for the immediate return of stolen land to the peasants and the expropriation of large estates. It declared Madero a traitor to the revolutionary cause and demanded that he be removed from office. In place of Madero, Zapata and his followers sought a more radical leader who would prioritize the needs of the rural poor and implement sweeping land reforms.

The Plan de Ayala resonated with many rural Mexicans, particularly in the south, where the concentration of land in the hands of a few wealthy families had left millions of peasants destitute. Zapata's forces, known as the Zapatistas, became one of the most formidable revolutionary armies, fighting not only against the remnants of Díaz's regime but also against Madero's government, which they viewed as insufficiently committed to the goals of the revolution.

Zapata's movement was deeply rooted in local traditions of communal land ownership, known as *ejidos*, which had existed in Mexico prior to the liberal reforms of the nineteenth century. The restoration of these communal lands was a central demand of the Plan de Ayala, and it became a rallying cry for the peasants who joined Zapata's army. While Madero's government sought to modernize Mexico through political reform,

Zapata's movement represented a more fundamental challenge to the country's social and economic order, calling for a return to a more egalitarian form of land ownership.

Zapata's break with Madero and the issuance of the Plan de Ayala set the stage for a new phase of the Mexican Revolution, in which the question of land reform would become a central issue. While Madero's presidency represented a brief attempt to establish a moderate, democratic government, the demands of revolutionary leaders like Zapata revealed the deeper social and economic divisions that the revolution had unleashed. The fight for land and economic justice would continue to drive the revolution long after Madero's death, as various factions vied for control of Mexico's future.

Ultimately, the rise of Emiliano Zapata and the Plan de Ayala represented a turning point in the revolution, shifting the focus from political reform to more radical demands for social and economic change. This shift would lead to a protracted and bloody struggle between different revolutionary factions, each with its own vision of what the revolution should achieve.

FALL OF MADERO AND HUERTA

"He who serves a revolution plows the sea."

— *SIMÓN BOLÍVAR*

THE RISE OF VICTORIANO HUERTA REPRESENTS ONE OF the darkest chapters in the Mexican Revolution. A military general with a reputation for ruthlessness, Huerta played a central role in the coup that toppled Francisco Madero, plunging the country back into chaos and violence. His betrayal of Madero and subsequent seizure of power in 1913 ignited a new and even more intense phase of the revolution, as various revolutionary factions united in opposition to his brutal dictatorship.

After Madero's election to the presidency in 1911, he faced many challenges. Despite being hailed as the leader who had ousted Porfirio Díaz, Madero's moderate approach to reform left many revolutionaries disillusioned. His refused to implement sweeping land reforms or dismantle the power structures that had been built up under Díaz. His reluctance to alienate the wealthy landowners and political elites who had supported Díaz created resentment among key revolutionary leaders such as Emiliano Zapata and Pancho Villa. Meanwhile, his decision to retain many of Díaz's military leaders in their positions further eroded his support.

Victoriano Huerta, one of the generals who had served under Díaz, remained in a powerful position within the military during Madero's presidency. Initially, Madero had hoped to rely on the military to maintain order and suppress ongoing insurgencies, including those led by Zapata in the south. However, Huerta's ambitions for power soon became evident. Working in collusion with conservative forces that sought to preserve the old order, including remnants of the Díaz regime and foreign interests, Huerta plotted to overthrow Madero.

In February 1913, Huerta carried out his plan, a coup known as the *Decena Trágica* (Ten Tragic Days), during which Mexico City was engulfed in violence. The coup began with a rebellion led by Félix Díaz, a relative of the former dictator, and General Bernardo Reyes, both of whom opposed Madero's government. Huerta, who had been entrusted by Madero to quell the rebellion, betrayed him by secretly aligning with the rebels. On February 18, 1913, Huerta arrested Madero and his vice president, José Suárez. A few days later, on February 22, both Madero and Suárez were assassinated on Huerta's orders, an act that shocked the nation and cemented Huerta's reputation as a cold-blooded opportunist.

Huerta's betrayal of Madero and the brutal murder of the president marked a decisive turning point in the revolution. The assassination of Madero, a symbol of hope for democratic reform, enraged many Mexicans who had supported the revolution, and it galvanized opposition to Huerta's regime. With Madero out of the picture, Huerta declared himself president and established a dictatorship characterized by repression, authoritarianism, and an open disregard for democratic institutions.

Huerta's regime quickly moved to consolidate power, using the military to crush any dissent. Political opponents were jailed or executed, and civil liberties were suspended. Huerta's authoritarian rule bore many similarities to the Porfiriato under Díaz, leading many Mexicans to view his rise as an attempt to restore the old order. Huerta's reign, however, was short-lived, as his brutal tactics and the widespread opposition he faced would soon lead to his downfall.

One of the unintended consequences of Huerta's dictatorship was that it united the previously fractured revolutionary factions in opposition to his rule. Leaders who had been bitter rivals during the early years of the revolution—such as Venustiano Carranza, Pancho Villa, and Emiliano Zapata—now found common cause in their desire to overthrow Huerta and restore constitutional governance to Mexico.

Venustiano Carranza, a wealthy landowner and politician from the state of Coahuila, emerged as one of the key figures in the fight against Huerta. Carranza had initially supported Madero during the revolution, and after Madero's assassination, he took up the mantle of leadership. In 1913, he issued the *Plan de Guadalupe*, a manifesto that declared Huerta's government illegitimate and called for the formation of a constitutional army to remove him from power. Carranza's Constitutionalist Army quickly became the leading force in the struggle against Huerta, attracting support from various revolutionary factions across the country.

Pancho Villa, who had been operating as a military leader in northern Mexico, also joined the opposition to Huerta. Villa's forces, known as the *División del Norte* (Division of the North), were highly mobile and effective, capable of striking quickly and decisively at Huerta's army. Villa's charisma and his ability to command the loyalty of his troops made him a formidable force in the fight against the dictatorship.

Meanwhile, in the south, Emiliano Zapata continued his struggle for land reform and social justice. Although Zapata had broken with Madero due to the latter's failure to implement significant land redistribution, he viewed Huerta as a far greater threat to the revolutionary cause. Zapata's forces, the Zapatistas, launched guerrilla campaigns against Huerta's army, particularly in the state of Morelos, where Zapata's demand for land reform remained central to the revolutionary struggle.

The alliance between Carranza, Villa, and Zapata was an uneasy one, as each leader had different visions for Mexico's future. Carranza, representing the more conservative, constitutionalist wing of the revolution, was primarily concerned with restoring democratic governance and political stability. Villa and Zapata, on the other hand, were more focused on addressing the social and economic inequalities that had fueled the revolution, particularly the issues of land reform and workers' rights. Despite these differences, the common goal of defeating Huerta united them, at least temporarily.

In addition to the internal opposition Huerta faced, his regime also encountered pressure from the United States. The U.S. government, under Woodrow Wilson, refused to recognize Huerta's government and imposed diplomatic and economic sanctions in an effort to undermine his rule. In April 1914, tensions between Huerta's government and the United States escalated into a military confrontation when U.S. forces occupied the port city of Veracruz. This intervention, combined with the growing strength of the revolutionary forces, weakened Huerta's grip on power and hastened his downfall.

As the revolutionary forces gained momentum, several key battles marked the decline of Huerta's dictatorship. One of the most significant of these was the Battle of Zacatecas, which took place in June 1914. Zacatecas was a strategically important city, and Huerta had fortified it heavily in an attempt to prevent Villa's forces from advancing further south. The city's capture was seen as essential for the revolutionary forces to gain control of central Mexico.

The Battle of Zacatecas was a pivotal moment in the Mexican Revolution, and Pancho Villa's use of innovative tactics played a crucial role in securing victory. Villa's forces executed advanced flanking techniques, sending smaller units to attack Huerta's forces from multiple directions. This not only stretched the defenders' lines thin but also created confusion among Huerta's ranks, making it difficult for them to organize a cohesive defense.

Villa understood the significance of Zacatecas' mountainous terrain and utilized it to his advantage. His troops secured high-ground positions, allowing them to fire down on Huerta's forces and maintain a superior vantage point throughout the battle. Controlling the high ground gave Villa's forces a significant tactical edge in terms of both defense and offense.

One of Villa's most significant innovations was his use of coordinated artillery fire. He combined the firepower of heavy artillery with the mobility of his cavalry forces, using sustained bombardments to soften enemy positions before sending in waves of infantry and cavalry to overwhelm them. The intensity of the artillery barrage demoralized Huerta's troops, contributing to the collapse of their defense.

Villa's División del Norte cavalry was known for its speed and agility, which allowed them to outmaneuver the enemy and strike at weak points in Huerta's defenses. Villa's cavalry could rapidly reposition to reinforce weak areas of attack or take advantage of breakthroughs, making his army highly adaptable during the battle.

In addition to physical military strategies, Villa employed psychological tactics, including the use of propaganda and rumors to lower the morale of Huerta's forces. His reputation as an unstoppable revolutionary leader preceded him, causing many of Huerta's soldiers to desert or surrender before the fighting reached its peak.

Villa's forces vastly outnumbered the defending troops in Zacatecas, with over twenty thousand men at his command. The sheer scale of his army allowed him to launch relentless assaults from multiple directions, overwhelming the defenders who were outnumbered and outgunned.

These innovative tactics not only ensured Villa's

victory at Zacatecas but also demonstrated his strategic prowess, helping to turn the tide of the Mexican Revolution in favor of the revolutionaries. The fall of Zacatecas was a severe blow to Huerta's regime and marked a crucial turning point in the revolution.

Following the defeat at Zacatecas, Huerta's position became increasingly untenable. His army was in disarray, his support among the elites was eroding, and the pressure from both revolutionary forces and the United States was mounting. In July 1914, less than a year and a half after seizing power, Huerta resigned from the presidency and fled into exile. He eventually sought refuge in Europe, much like Porfirio Díaz before him, and later died in the United States in 1916.

Huerta's fall from power marked the end of one phase of the Mexican Revolution, but it did not bring an end to the conflict. The revolutionary factions that had united to overthrow Huerta soon turned against each other, as Carranza, Villa, and Zapata vied for control of Mexico's future. Nevertheless, Huerta's ousting was a significant victory for the revolutionaries, as it demonstrated the ability of diverse and often antagonistic factions to come together in the face of a common enemy. His departure also cleared the way for the next phase of the revolution, in which the battle for control of the country would shift from a fight against dictatorship to a struggle over the shape of the new political and social order.

FIGHTING FOR CONTROL

"I would rather die on my feet than live on my knees."

— *EMILIANO ZAPATA*

THE FALL OF HUERTA IN JULY 1914 MARKED THE END OF his short-lived dictatorship, but it did not bring peace to Mexico. Instead, the revolution entered a new and even more violent phase, as the various revolutionary factions that had united against Huerta now turned on each other in a fierce struggle for control of the country. The power vacuum created by Huerta's departure intensified the internal divisions within the revolutionary movement, leading to a civil war that pitted three main leaders against each other: Venustiano Carranza, Pancho Villa, and Emiliano Zapata.

Each of these leaders represented different constituencies and had different visions for Mexico's future. The collapse of the common enemy in Huerta allowed these underlying differences to come to the fore again. What had once been a broadly united movement against dictatorship now fractured into a multi-sided conflict over the direction of the revolution and the shape of Mexico's new political and social order.

Pancho Villa, the charismatic leader of the División del Norte (Division of the North), was primarily focused on regional autonomy and addressing the needs of the rural poor, especially in northern Mexico. Villa's army, which had played a critical role in defeating Huerta, consisted largely of landless peasants, former laborers, and soldiers who had been marginalized under both Díaz and Huerta. Villa believed that the revolution should bring about significant social and economic reforms, particularly land redistribution, to improve the lives of the working classes. He also advocated for regional governance, which would allow northern Mexico to maintain a degree of independence from the central government in Mexico City.

In contrast, Emiliano Zapata, who led the Zapatistas in southern Mexico, was singularly focused on land reform. For Zapata and his followers, the revolution was about returning land to the peasants who had been dispossessed by large landowners and the expansion of the hacienda system. Zapata's Plan de Ayala, issued in 1911, had called for the immediate expropriation of land from wealthy landowners and its redistribution to the rural poor. Unlike Villa, Zapata's vision was less concerned with political power or national governance and more focused on achieving economic justice for Mexico's rural population, particularly in his home state of Morelos. For Zapata, the revolution was incomplete until land reform was fully realized.

Carranza, the leader of the Constitutionalist Army,

represented a more conservative wing of the revolutionary movement. Carranza, a wealthy landowner from Coahuila, had initially joined the revolution to overthrow Díaz and later Huerta, but his primary goal was to establish a centralized, constitutional government. Carranza was not as concerned with land reform as Villa and Zapata; instead, he sought to restore order and create a stable political system based on democratic institutions and the rule of law. His vision for Mexico was more focused on political and legal reforms than on the social and economic changes demanded by Villa and Zapata.

These divergent goals made cooperation between the three leaders difficult, if not impossible. While all three had fought against Huerta, they now found themselves in direct competition for control of the revolution. The tensions between them would soon erupt into open conflict, as each leader sought to impose his vision on the rest of the country.

After Huerta's fall, Carranza quickly moved to assert his authority over the revolutionary movement. As the leader of the Constitutionalist Army, Carranza had positioned himself as the defender of constitutionalism and the rule of law. His goal was to establish a centralized government that could bring stability to Mexico after years of civil war and political chaos. In this sense, Carranza's vision was more focused on political and institutional reforms than on the social and economic changes advocated by Villa and Zapata.

Carranza's rise to power was aided by his ability to navigate the political landscape and forge alliances with key military leaders. He was also able to gain the support of the United States, which had grown increasingly concerned about the instability in Mexico and was looking for a leader who could restore order and protect American economic interests. In 1915, the U.S. government officially recognized Carranza as the legitimate leader of Mexico, a move that strengthened his position and allowed him to consolidate power.

One of Carranza's most significant achievements was the drafting of the 1917 Constitution, a landmark document that sought to address many of the grievances that had fueled the revolution. The 1917 Constitution promised land reform, labor rights, and the nationalization of natural resources, marking a significant departure from the policies of previous regimes. Article 27 of the Constitution was particularly important, as it laid the groundwork for the expropriation of large estates and the redistribution of land to peasants. It also asserted that Mexico's natural resources, including its vast oil reserves, belonged to the nation and could not be owned by foreign interests.

In addition to land reform, the Constitution also included provisions to protect workers' rights. Article 123 established an eight-hour workday, the right to strike, and protections against child labor. These labor reforms were a response to the demands of urban workers who had played a key role in the revolutionary movement and sought greater protections in the workplace.

Despite these reforms, Carranza's presidency was marked by ongoing conflict with Villa and Zapata, both of whom remained distrustful of his intentions and continued to challenge his authority. While Carranza's Constitution promised land reform, in practice, its implementation was slow and uneven, particularly in the regions controlled by Villa and Zapata. For many of the rural poor, Carranza's government was seen as too conservative and too closely aligned with the interests of the wealthy landowners who had dominated Mexican politics for decades.

In the aftermath of Huerta's fall, Pancho Villa and Emiliano Zapata formed a temporary alliance in an effort to challenge Carranza's authority and impose their own vision of revolutionary reform. Despite their ideological differences, Villa and Zapata shared a common goal: to prevent Carranza from consolidating power and to ensure that the revolution resulted in meaningful social and economic change, particularly in the areas of land redistribution and workers' rights.

In December 1914, Villa and Zapata's forces occupied Mexico City, the symbolic heart of the country's political power. Their entry into the capital marked a high point in their alliance and a dramatic challenge to Carranza's government. Villa and Zapata hoped that by controlling Mexico City, they could pressure Carranza into accepting their demands for more radical reforms. However, their occupation of the capital was short-lived, and the alliance between Villa and Zapata soon began to unravel.

The main reason for the failure of their partnership was the fundamental difference in their visions for Mexico's future. Villa, with his stronghold in the north, was more focused on regional autonomy and military dominance, while Zapata remained committed to his plan for land reform in the south. Neither leader had a clear plan for governing the entire country, and their forces lacked the administrative capabilities needed to maintain control over Mexico City.

Moreover, Villa and Zapata were both regional leaders whose power bases were rooted in specific parts of the country. Villa's support came from the northern states, while Zapata's influence was concentrated in Morelos and other parts of southern Mexico. Their inability to form a cohesive national movement made it difficult for them to challenge Carranza's more centralized vision of governance.

In the end, Carranza was able to outmaneuver Villa and Zapata, both militarily and politically. With the support of the United States and a growing number of revolutionary factions that preferred a more stable and centralized government, Carranza's forces retook Mexico City in 1915. Villa and Zapata's brief occupation of the capital was over, and their alliance collapsed soon afterward.

Zapata returned to Morelos, where he continued his fight for land reform, while Villa retreated to the north, where he continued to wage guerrilla warfare against Carranza's forces. Both leaders would ultimately meet violent ends: Zapata was assassinated in 1919, while Villa was killed in 1923. Their deaths marked the end of an era in the Mexican Revolution, but their legacies—particularly their demands for land reform and social justice—would continue to shape Mexican politics for decades to come.

Carranza's victory in the struggle for control of the revolution was not absolute. While he succeeded in establishing a constitutional government and enacting important reforms, the revolution's underlying social and economic tensions remained unresolved. The demands of Villa, Zapata, and their followers for more radical change had been suppressed, but they had not been eradicated. In the years that followed, these tensions would continue to shape Mexico's political landscape, culminating in the rise of the Institutional Revolutionary Party (PRI), which would dominate Mexican politics for much of the twentieth century.

THE 1917 CONSTITUTION

"The land belongs to those who work it."

— EMILIANO ZAPATA

THE MEXICAN CONSTITUTION OF 1917 STANDS AS ONE OF the most transformative documents in the country's history, and its significance cannot be overstated. Drafted during a period of intense social upheaval, the Constitution was designed not only to address the political instability that had defined Mexico for decades but also to resolve many of the social and economic grievances that had fueled the revolution. It was an ambitious document that sought to reshape the nation's political and economic structures, and many of its provisions were groundbreaking for their time, particularly in their focus on labor rights, land reform, and the role of the state in national development.

The Constitution of 1917 is one of the most significant legal documents in Mexican history, and its key provisions laid the groundwork for the social, political, and economic structures of modern Mexico. Some of the important aspects of the Constitution were:

Land Ownership (Article 27)

Article 27 addressed one of the most pressing issues of the Mexican Revolution land reform. The article declared that all land and natural resources belong to the nation, giving the government the authority to expropriate land for public use, a significant move toward land redistribution. This provision led to the breakup of large estates (haciendas) and gave land to peasants, forming the foundation of Mexico's agrarian reform programs in the following decades. It also restricted foreign ownership of land, particularly in strategic areas such as borders and coastlines, aiming to reduce foreign influence over Mexican resources.

Workers' Rights (Article 123)

Article 123 was groundbreaking in its protection of labor rights. It established an eight-hour workday, the right to strike, and protections for women and children in the workforce. This article also guaranteed fair wages, rest days, and compensation for accidents or illness resulting from work. These provisions represented a huge victory for labor movements in Mexico and became a model for labor laws in other parts of Latin America. The article called for the establishment of labor courts, setting the precedent for government involvement in mediating disputes between workers and employers.

Separation of Church and State

The Constitution of 1917 included several provisions that aimed to drastically reduce the power and influence of the Catholic Church in Mexico. These were some of the most controversial articles and sparked ongoing tensions between the church and the government. Three of these were under Articles 3, 27, and 130.

- Article 3 mandated secular education in public schools, effectively removing the church's influence from the education system.
- Article 27 limited the church's ownership of land, allowing the state to seize properties held by religious institutions.
- Article 130 strictly limited the church's role in politics, prohibiting religious figures from holding public office, engaging in political campaigns, or criticizing the government.

These provisions were intended to break the historical dominance of the Catholic Church in Mexican society, a legacy of colonial rule, and created a secular state that emphasized the separation between religion and politics.

The Constitution of 1917 established democratic principles such as universal suffrage, ensuring that Mexican citizens could participate in the electoral process.

It also introduced direct elections for the president and other key government positions, attempting to prevent the type of autocratic rule that characterized the Porfirio Díaz era.

One of the significant reforms was the limitation on the president's power. The constitution prohibited re-election, aiming to curb the potential for dictatorships and ensure a transition of power, a lesson learned from Díaz's prolonged tenure.

In addition to the secular nature of education outlined in Article 3, the Constitution made the state responsible for providing free, compulsory, and secular education. This was part of a broader effort to modernize and democratize Mexico by educating the masses and reducing illiteracy, especially in rural areas.

The Constitution granted the Mexican government sovereignty over its natural resources, including oil. Article 27 played a crucial role in the eventual nationalization of the oil industry under President Cárdenas in 1938. This laid the foundation for Mexico's state-run oil company, PEMEX, and demonstrated Mexico's commitment to controlling its own economic destiny.

The Constitution of 1917 remains in effect today, although it has been amended numerous times to address the changing needs of Mexican society. It was seen as a progressive and radical document at the time, particularly with its provisions for social justice, labor rights, and land reform. Its emphasis on secularism, workers' rights, and land redistribution represented a break from the colonial and Porfirian past.

The constitution also symbolized the consolidation of the gains made during the Mexican Revolution and provided a legal framework to guide the country toward modernization, social equity, and political stability.

This constitution not only shaped the course of twentieth-century Mexico but also influenced other nations in Latin America seeking to address similar issues of inequality, labor rights, and the relationship between church and state.

One of the most important and controversial provisions was Article 27, which addressed land reform, an issue at the heart of the Mexican Revolution. Article 27 declared that the nation had the right to regulate the ownership and use of land to ensure that it served the public good. It asserted that all land, water, and natural resources within Mexico's borders ultimately belonged to the Mexican state. This provision paved the way for the expropriation of large estates (haciendas) and their redistribution to peasants, fulfilling one of the primary demands of Emiliano Zapata and other revolutionary leaders who had fought for the rights of the rural poor. The article also limited the amount of land that could be owned by foreign individuals or corporations, addressing the widespread foreign ownership of land that had been a hallmark of Porfirio Díaz's regime.

In practice, however, the implementation of land reform was slow and uneven. While the Constitution provided the legal framework for land redistribution, the actual process of expropriating land from wealthy landowners and distributing it to peasants took decades to fully realize. Still, Article 27 became a cornerstone of Mexican agrarian policy and symbolized the revolutionary commitment to social justice, even if its promises were not immediately fulfilled.

Another significant provision of the Constitution was Article 123, which addressed labor rights. This article was revolutionary in its protection of workers, particularly in an era when labor conditions were often brutal and exploitative. Article 123 established an eight-hour workday, provided for a day of rest each week, mandated equal pay for equal work regardless of gender, and allowed workers the right to unionize and strike. It also prohibited child labor and created a framework for workers to receive compensation for workplace injuries.

The inclusion of labor rights in the Constitution was a direct response to the demands of urban workers who had played a significant role in the revolutionary movement. Mexico's growing industrial workforce had suffered under exploitative conditions for decades, and the Constitution aimed to provide them with greater protections and opportunities. Like the provisions for land reform, the labor reforms outlined in Article 123 were not always fully implemented in the immediate aftermath of the revolution, but they laid the groundwork for future labor legislation and union activism in Mexico.

The separation of church and state was another key principle enshrined in the 1917 Constitution. The relationship between the Catholic Church and the Mexican government had been a contentious issue for much of the country's history, and the Constitution sought to limit the power and influence of the Church in public life. Under the Constitution, the government took control of many church properties and restricted the Church's ability to operate schools or hold large amounts of land. The secularization of education was also a major goal of the new government, as it sought to create a public education system free from religious influence.

The restrictions placed on the Catholic Church by the 1917 Constitution would lead to significant tension between the government and the Church, culminating in the Cristero War of the late 1920s, a violent uprising by conservative Catholics who opposed the secularization efforts of the post-revolutionary government. Despite this resistance, the principles of secularism and the separation of church and state became foundational elements of modern Mexican governance.

Following the adoption of the 1917 Constitution, Venustiano Carranza, who had been instrumental in its drafting, assumed the presidency and sought to implement its provisions. Carranza's presidency was marked by both progress and significant challenges, as he tried to navigate the deep divisions that remained within the revolutionary movement.

Carranza, though a key figure in the revolution, was not universally loved. His vision for Mexico's future, which emphasized a centralized government and a return to political stability, often clashed with the more radical elements of the revolutionary coalition. While the Constitution he helped draft promised significant reforms, Carranza's government was slow to implement them, particularly in terms of land redistribution. This reluctance alienated many of his former allies, including Pancho Villa and Emiliano Zapata, who had fought for more immediate and drastic changes.

The slow pace of reform under Carranza's leadership, particularly with regard to land, created a deep sense of frustration among revolutionary factions. Zapata, who had always been skeptical of Carranza's commitment to land reform, continued his insurgency in southern Mexico, advocating for the immediate implementation of the Plan de Ayala. Villa, too, remained a thorn in Carranza's side, leading armed uprisings in the north. Carranza's presidency became defined by his efforts to consolidate power in the face of these ongoing rebellions, as well as his attempts to build a functioning government based on the principles of the new Constitution.

Internally, Carranza faced opposition even from within his own ranks. The revolutionary movement had been a broad coalition of various groups, and as president, Carranza struggled to keep these factions united. His refusal to compromise with Villa and Zapata, combined with his efforts to maintain a degree of order and stability, ultimately led to the fragmentation of the revolutionary alliance.

ASSASSINATIONS OF VILLA AND ZAPATA

"They thought they were killing men, but they were killing ideas."

— *ANONYMOUS*

THE ASSASSINATIONS OF EMILIANO ZAPATA AND PANCHO Villa marked the end of two of the most prominent figures of the Mexican Revolution and signaled the consolidation of power under Carranza's successors. Both men had come to symbolize the more radical elements of the revolution, particularly in their demands for land reform and social justice. Their deaths were a clear indication that the revolutionary leadership was moving away from the radical goals that had driven much of the early revolutionary fervor.

Emiliano Zapata's assassination on April 10, 1919, was a carefully orchestrated betrayal that ultimately sealed the fate of one of the Mexican Revolution's most iconic leaders. For years, Zapata had led a powerful insurgency in southern Mexico, fighting for the rights of peasants and indigenous people who had been oppressed under the harsh hacienda system. His movement was rooted in the principle of *Tierra y Libertad* (Land and Liberty), and he had gathered a loyal following among those who yearned for land reform and a better future. But Zapata's radical vision for Mexico put him at odds with powerful figures, particularly Venustiano Carranza, who saw him as a threat to the fragile stability he was trying to build after years of revolutionary turmoil.

By 1919, Zapata's forces had become a significant obstacle to Carranza's plans. While both men had fought against the oppressive regime of Victoriano Huerta, their visions for post-revolutionary Mexico could not have been more different. Zapata wanted sweeping agrarian reform, while Carranza favored a more conservative approach, focusing on maintaining the existing order and modernizing the nation without fully dismantling the power structures that had long oppressed Mexico's rural population. Zapata's refusal to compromise on his ideals, along with his growing influence in southern Mexico, convinced Carranza that the revolutionary leader had to be eliminated.

To accomplish this, Carranza's government devised a cunning plan. Colonel Jesús Guajardo, a local Carrancista officer, was tasked with luring Zapata into a deadly trap. Guajardo, posing as a disgruntled officer who was willing to defect to Zapata's side, reached out to the revolutionary leader with promises of an alliance. He claimed to support Zapata's cause and, to gain his trust, even staged a fake mutiny, executing several government soldiers as proof of his loyalty. Zapata, always looking for ways to strengthen his forces and further his cause, decided to meet with Guajardo to discuss the potential alliance.

The meeting was arranged at the Hacienda de San Juan Chinameca, near Cuautla in the state of Morelos. On the morning of April 10, 1919, Zapata, accompanied by a small group of his men, rode to the hacienda, unaware of the treachery that awaited him. As he arrived, Guajardo's men greeted him with the respect and deference reserved for a revolutionary leader. Zapata dismounted his horse, unaware that hidden gunmen had taken positions inside the hacienda's walls.

As Zapata entered the courtyard, Guajardo's soldiers, who had been waiting for the signal, opened fire. Zapata was shot multiple times, and his body fell to the ground. The man who had come to symbolize the fight for land reform and the rights of the oppressed had been cut down in a brutal ambush. His men, stunned and outnumbered, were forced to retreat.

The assassination of Emiliano Zapata was not just the death of a man; it was a devastating blow to the revolutionary movement in southern Mexico. With Zapata gone, the hope for immediate, radical land reform under Carranza's government faded. While Zapata's ideals lived on, inspiring future agrarian movements and policies in Mexico, the revolutionary momentum that he had built was severely weakened. For the peasants who had followed him, it was a dark day, signaling the end of their most passionate and uncompromising advocate.

Zapata's death sent shockwaves through the country. His supporters mourned not only the loss of their leader but also the loss of their dream for a Mexico where land was truly redistributed to the people. Carranza, for his part, believed he had removed a major obstacle to his control, but he underestimated the enduring power of Zapata's legacy. Though he was gone, Zapata became a martyr for the cause of land reform, and his image and ideals would continue to inspire generations of Mexicans long after his death.

The assassination of Pancho Villa on July 20, 1923, marked the violent end of yet another iconic figure from the Mexican Revolution. Villa, much like Emiliano Zapata, had been a symbol of the revolutionary struggle, especially in the northern regions of Mexico, where his daring raids and guerrilla warfare had made him a legend. After years of leading a fierce insurgency and commanding his formidable División del Norte, Villa had finally laid down his arms and retreated from the political spotlight. He retired to a ranch in Canutillo, Chihuahua, content to live a quieter life away from the chaos that had defined his earlier years.

Despite stepping away from active rebellion, Villa's name continued to resonate across Mexico. His popularity, particularly among the poor and those who had benefited from his redistribution of wealth and land, made him an ever-present figure in the political landscape. Villa had always been a divisive character—beloved by many, feared by others—and the mere fact that he was still alive posed a potential threat to the new post-revolutionary government led by President Álvaro Obregón (elected in 1920). Villa's charismatic leadership, coupled with his military successes during the revolution, left many in power uneasy about his potential to stir unrest or even lead a new rebellion, should the political winds shift.

It was under this cloud of suspicion that a plan was hatched to remove Villa once and for all. On July 20, 1923, Villa set out on what seemed to be a routine journey. He was traveling by car through the town of Parral, Chihuahua, accompanied by a few bodyguards and close associates. Villa, having grown accustomed to his new life of relative peace, was not expecting any danger on this day, but the quiet streets of Parral soon became the scene of a deadly ambush.

As Villa's car passed through the town, gunmen who had been lying in wait opened fire. The ambush was swift and brutal. Villa's car was riddled with bullets, and he was struck multiple times, killing him almost instantly. Several of his companions were also killed in the attack, while a few managed to survive. The attack was meticulously planned, leaving little doubt that it had been orchestrated by agents of the government. Villa's death, much like Zapata's, was a carefully calculated move to eliminate a revolutionary figure whose very existence threatened the fragile stability of the newly established political order.

Villa's assassination sent shockwaves throughout Mexico. For many, it was the end of an era. The two towering figures of the revolution, Zapata and Villa, were now both gone. With their deaths, the revolutionary fervor that had once gripped the country began to subside, allowing the post-revolutionary leadership to consolidate power and focus on building a centralized, more stable government.

Villa's legacy, however, was far from forgotten. Much like Zapata, Villa became a symbol of resistance and defiance against the entrenched powers that had long oppressed the Mexican people. His actions during the revolution—redistributing wealth, challenging the powerful, and fighting for the underdog—cemented his place in the hearts of many Mexicans. Although he had lived the final years of his life in relative peace, his assassination was a stark reminder that, even in death, Pancho Villa was seen as a threat to the new order.

Villa's passing also marked the beginning of a period of political calm, as the revolutionary leadership, no longer facing the internal divisions represented by figures like Villa and Zapata, turned their attention to solidifying their control over Mexico. The violence and chaos of the revolution were gradually replaced by efforts to modernize the country and implement the social and economic reforms that had been at the heart of the revolutionary struggle. Yet, for many, the loss of Villa was a bittersweet moment—a recognition that, while the revolution had succeeded in many ways, the era of radical leaders willing to challenge the status quo had come to an end.

The assassinations of Zapata and Villa cleared the way for Carranza's successors, including Álvaro Obregón and Plutarco Elías Calles, to establish a new political order in Mexico. These leaders would continue the process of implementing the reforms promised in the 1917 Constitution, but the radical spirit of the revolution had been tempered. The focus shifted toward political stability and economic development, with the most far-reaching land and labor reforms being implemented more gradually over the course of the twentieth century.

In the end, the 1917 Constitution and the deaths of

Villa and Zapata signaled the end of the revolutionary phase in Mexican history and the beginning of the post-revolutionary state. While the revolution did not achieve all of its goals immediately, the Constitution provided the framework for future reforms, and the legacy of the revolution continued to shape Mexican politics and society for decades to come.

CONSEQUENCES AND GLOBAL IMPACT

"This revolution has come to an end, but there are many things still to be done."

— *VENUSTIANO CARRANZA*

THE MEXICAN REVOLUTION HAD PROFOUND AND devastating immediate consequences for Mexico. It was one of the most violent conflicts in the country's history, and the toll it took on the Mexican population was staggering. By the time the dust settled, it was estimated that between one and two million people had lost their lives due to the war. This number included not only soldiers and combatants but also civilians who were caught in the crossfire, displaced, or killed by disease and famine exacerbated by the conflict.

The revolution displaced vast numbers of Mexicans, both within the country and beyond its borders. Entire villages were destroyed, and large swaths of the population were forced to flee their homes in search of safety. Many fled to the United States, where they sought refuge from the violence. These waves of migration had a significant impact on both Mexico and the U.S., particularly in the border regions, where populations surged, and Mexican communities began to reshape the cultural and social landscape of American cities.

Economically, the revolution left Mexico in a state of ruin. The agricultural sector, already strained under the hacienda system, was decimated by the violence, as many of the country's most productive farmlands were abandoned or destroyed during the fighting. Industrial output also plummeted as factories and infrastructure were damaged, and foreign investors withdrew their capital. Additionally, the revolutionary factions often resorted to looting and confiscating property to fund their campaigns, further weakening the already fragile economy. Inflation soared, and many Mexicans found themselves struggling to survive in a country ravaged by years of civil war.

The social structure of Mexico was also deeply affected by the revolution. While the *hacendados* (large landowners) had dominated the country for centuries, the revolution severely weakened their grip on power. Many of the haciendas were broken up or abandoned, and the revolution created a new class of small landowners, as some of the promises of land redistribution began to take effect, particularly after the enactment of the 1917 Constitution. The middle class, which had been growing prior to the revolution, found itself in a precarious position. Although some members of the middle class gained power and influence through the revolutionary movement, others saw their fortunes dwindle due to the economic instability and political uncertainty that followed the conflict.

For the peasantry and working class, the immediate aftermath of the revolution brought mixed results. While the promises of land reform and labor rights were enshrined in the new Constitution, the reality was that these changes took time to be fully realized. Many peasants remained landless, and workers continued to face difficult conditions. However, the revolution had planted the seeds for future reforms, and over the next several decades, Mexico would slowly begin to implement the changes that the revolution had promised.

One of the most significant long-term consequences of the Mexican Revolution was its impact on the country's political structure. The revolution fundamentally altered the way Mexico was governed, leading to the creation of a new political system that would dominate the country for much of the twentieth century. This system was centered around the emergence of the Institutional Revolutionary Party (PRI), a political organization that grew out of the revolutionary movement and became the dominant force in Mexican politics for over seventy years.

The PRI, originally founded as the National Revolutionary Party (PNR) in 1929, was the brainchild of Plutarco Elías Calles, one of the key revolutionary leaders who sought to stabilize the country after the chaos of the revolution. The party was designed to unify the various factions of the revolution and create a system of institutionalized political succession, thereby preventing the kind of violent power struggles that had characterized the revolution itself. Over time, the PRI evolved into a powerful political machine that controlled nearly every aspect of Mexican political life.

One of the defining characteristics of the PRI was

its ability to incorporate various elements of Mexican society, including labor unions, peasant organizations, and business interests, into its structure. This allowed the party to maintain a broad base of support and remain in power for decades. The PRI's dominance was also facilitated by its use of patronage, clientelism, and, at times, electoral fraud to maintain control over the political system. While the PRI presented itself as the guardian of the revolution's ideals, in practice, it often prioritized political stability and economic growth over the more radical social and economic reforms that had been promised during the revolution.

Despite these shortcomings, the PRI did oversee significant changes in Mexico, particularly in terms of land reform and labor rights. Under PRI rule, the Mexican government implemented a series of agrarian reforms that redistributed land to peasants, although these reforms were often limited in scope and did not fully address the inequalities that had fueled the revolution. The PRI also worked to improve the conditions of urban workers, particularly through its close relationship with labor unions. However, the party's conservative approach to governance often frustrated those who had hoped for more radical change.

The PRI remained in power until the year 2000, when it finally lost the presidency to the opposition candidate Vicente Fox of the National Action Party (PAN). Despite its eventual decline, the PRI's legacy as the political heir to the revolution left an indelible mark on Mexican politics. The party's ability to maintain control for so long is a testament to its success in institutionalizing the revolution and creating a system of governance that, while not always democratic or responsive to the needs of the people, was remarkably stable in the context of Mexico's turbulent history.

The Mexican Revolution had far-reaching consequences beyond the borders of Mexico, influencing revolutionary movements across Latin America and beyond. As one of the first major social revolutions of the twentieth century, the Mexican Revolution set a precedent for other movements that sought to challenge entrenched power structures and address issues of inequality, land reform, and labor rights. Its impact was particularly significant in Latin America, where similar social and economic conditions existed in many countries.

One of the key ways in which the Mexican Revolution influenced other movements was through its focus on land reform. The issue of land ownership was a central theme of the revolution, and the redistribution of land to peasants became a rallying cry for revolutionary leaders like Emiliano Zapata. This emphasis on land reform resonated with other countries in Latin America, where large landowners controlled much of the arable land, and the rural poor were left with little or no access to resources. The success of the Mexican Revolution in addressing this issue, at least in principle, inspired later land reform movements in countries such as Bolivia, Guatemala, and Peru.

The revolution also had a significant impact on the broader struggle in Latin America. During the revolution, foreign intervention, particularly by the United States, played a significant role in shaping the course of events. The U.S. had extensive economic interests in Mexico, particularly in the mining and oil sectors, and it frequently intervened to protect these interests. The U.S.

occupation of Veracruz in 1914 and its support for various revolutionary factions demonstrated the extent to which foreign powers were willing to influence the outcome of the revolution. For many Latin American countries, the Mexican Revolution became a symbol of resistance against foreign domination, and its leaders were seen as champions of national sovereignty.

Globally, the Mexican Revolution served as an early example of a social revolution that sought to address deep-rooted inequalities in land ownership and labor rights. In this sense, it can be seen as a precursor to later revolutionary movements, including the Russian Revolution of 1917, which also focused on the redistribution of land and the rights of workers. While the Mexican Revolution was not as ideologically driven as the Russian Revolution, the two shared common themes of social justice and the need to address economic disparities.

The Mexican Revolution also influenced intellectual and artistic movements around the world. The revolution's ideals of social justice and national identity inspired a generation of artists, writers, and thinkers, both within Mexico and abroad. Figures such as Diego Rivera, Frida Kahlo, and José Clemente Orozco used their art to depict the struggles of the Mexican people and the ideals of the revolution, creating a powerful visual language that resonated beyond Mexico's borders.

In summary, the Mexican Revolution had both immediate and long-term consequences that reshaped Mexico's political, social, and economic landscape. Its impact was felt not only within Mexico but also across Latin America and the world, where it inspired revolutionary movements and intellectual currents. The revolution's legacy, particularly in terms of land reform and labor rights, continues to influence Mexican politics and society to this day. Although the promises of the revolution were not fully realized in the years following the conflict, the ideals it espoused—justice, equality, and national sovereignty—remain central to Mexico's national identity.

LESSONS FROM THE REVOLUTION

"Tierra y Libertad" (Land and Liberty)

— THE MOTTO OF EMILIANO ZAPATA

THE MEXICAN REVOLUTION WAS A TRANSFORMATIVE event in the country's history, marking the end of Porfirio Díaz's thirty-five-year dictatorship and ushering in a new political and social order. What began as a movement to overthrow Díaz's authoritarian regime quickly evolved into a complex and violent struggle between various revolutionary factions, each with its own vision for Mexico's future. The revolution introduced significant reforms that would reshape Mexican society, most notably through the 1917 Constitution, which laid the groundwork for land redistribution, labor rights, and the separation of church and state.

While the revolution succeeded in toppling Díaz, it also led to years of civil war and internal conflict as leaders like Francisco Madero, Emiliano Zapata, Pancho Villa, and Venustiano Carranza vied for control of the country. The deaths of Zapata and Villa, coupled with the rise of the Institutional Revolutionary Party (PRI), marked the consolidation of power in post-revolutionary Mexico

One of the key takeaways is the difficulty of translating revolutionary ideals into practical reforms. While the 1917 Constitution enshrined significant promises of land and labor reform, the reality of implementing these changes was fraught with obstacles, including resistance from powerful landowners and internal divisions within the revolutionary factions.

The revolution also highlights the dangers of factionalism in revolutionary movements. Although many of the revolutionary leaders initially united against a common enemy in Díaz and later Huerta, their differing visions for the country's future eventually led to bitter conflict. Factionalism within the revolution not only prolonged the violence but also complicated efforts to enact meaningful reforms. The struggles between leaders like Villa, Zapata, and Carranza underscore the complexities of maintaining unity in a revolutionary movement, particularly when differing ideologies and regional interests are at play.

Finally, the Mexican Revolution serves as a reminder of the complexity of revolutionary change. While revolutions often promise swift and radical transformations, the reality is that such change takes time and is often met with resistance from entrenched interests. The slow and uneven implementation of the reforms outlined in the 1917 Constitution illustrates the challenges of creating a new social order while maintaining balance, even in the wake of a successful revolution.

The legacy of the Mexican Revolution can be seen

in the broader trends of the twentieth century, particularly in the rise of nationalism, the struggle for social justice, and anti-colonial movements around the world. The revolution was one of the first major social upheavals of the twentieth century, and it set a precedent for other revolutionary movements, particularly in Latin America, where issues of land reform, workers' rights, and national sovereignty were central to political struggles.

The Mexican Revolution also parallels other global movements for independence and social reform, such as the Russian Revolution in 1917 and the later anti-colonial movements in Africa and Asia. Like these other movements, the Mexican Revolution was driven by a desire to break free from foreign domination, address social and economic inequalities, and create a more just and equitable society. The revolution's emphasis on land reform, in particular, resonated with other countries where rural populations had long been marginalized by elite landowners and foreign interests.

As we reflect on the Mexican Revolution, it is clear that its impact extends far beyond the borders of Mexico. It was a revolutionary movement that not only reshaped the country's political and social landscape but also influenced revolutionary thought around the world. The ideals of social justice, land reform, and national sovereignty that emerged from the revolution continue to shape modern Mexico and have left a lasting legacy in Latin American history.

Looking ahead, it is worth considering how the lessons of the Mexican Revolution apply to other revolutionary movements and struggles across the globe.

Their revolution's successes and failures offer valuable insights into the complexities of enacting change in deeply entrenched systems.

PORFIRIO DÍAZ

Fig 1

José de la Cruz Porfirio Díaz Mori ruled
Mexico for over three decades, from 1876 until 1911,
and his authoritarian grip on power ultimately set the
stage for the Mexican Revolution. Known as the "Porfiriato," his long tenure was marked by a focus on

modernization, foreign investment, and industrial growth, but these advancements came at a steep cost. While Díaz brought stability to a country plagued by political chaos, the methods he used to maintain control —favoring the wealthy elite, suppressing dissent, and marginalizing the rural and indigenous populations— created deep social and economic inequalities that would lead to his eventual downfall.

Porfirio Díaz, born in Oaxaca in 1830, first rose to prominence as a military leader. He gained national attention for his role in the Battle of Puebla during the French Intervention in Mexico in 1862, where Mexican forces famously defeated the French army. Díaz leveraged his military success and popularity to enter politics, and in 1876, after leading a rebellion against President Sebastián Lerdo de Tejada, he seized the presidency.

Díaz initially presented himself as a defender of democracy, claiming he would uphold Mexico's liberal constitution and restore order. However, his early promises to respect democratic principles quickly faded as he consolidated power. By the early 1880s, Díaz had become the de facto dictator of Mexico, ruling through a combination of political manipulation, cronyism, and outright repression.

The Porfiriato era saw tremendous economic development, particularly in infrastructure. Railroads crisscrossed the country, factories sprung up in major cities, and foreign investment poured into sectors like mining and agriculture. Díaz's government promoted modernization and industrialization, seeing them as the keys to transforming Mexico into a modern nation.

However, this progress was unevenly distributed.

The benefits of modernization primarily went to a small group of elites—landowners, industrialists, and foreign investors—while the majority of Mexicans, particularly peasants and indigenous communities, saw their lands taken over by large estates (haciendas) and foreign companies. Under Díaz, the system of encomiendas and large landholdings expanded, leaving many rural Mexicans landless and impoverished. The government expropriated communal lands, forcing indigenous people to work on large haciendas or in industrial settings under harsh conditions.

Díaz maintained his power through a complex system of patronage and political alliances. He hand-picked governors, judges, and local officials, ensuring that loyalty to his regime remained strong. Dissent was ruthlessly crushed, and opposition leaders were either co-opted or silenced. The famous slogan of the Díaz regime, "Pan o Palo" (Bread or the Club), reflected his approach—reward compliance, punish resistance.

His rule consisted of three periods, each longer than the previous. On November 28, 1876, he became provisional president when José Maria Iglesias went into exile. After eight days, Díaz appointed Juan N. Méndez substitute president while Díaz went to fight the supporters of Lerdo de Tejada in the Battle of Tecoac. Mendez remained substitute president for seventy-three days, after which Díaz reassumed office. On May 5, 1877, Congress appointed him constitutional president.

After four years, Díaz lost the general election of 1880 to Manuel González Flores. Flores's presidency lasted another four years. Díaz then won the rigged 1884 general election, receiving 98.8% of the vote, and didn't relinquish his office until 1911.

As Díaz's rule extended into the early twentieth century, opposition began to grow, especially among the middle class, intellectuals, and rural poor. The gap between rich and poor widened, and dissatisfaction simmered beneath the surface. In 1908, Díaz made a fateful error in an interview with U.S. journalist James Creelman. He suggested that he would step down from power and allow free elections, implying that Mexico was ready for democracy. This statement encouraged opposition figures like Francisco Madero, who declared his candidacy for the presidency in 1910.

When Díaz reneged on his promise and rigged the election to maintain power, Madero called for an armed uprising. On November 20, 1910, Madero's call for revolution sparked what would become the Mexican Revolution, a decade-long conflict that would ultimately reshape the country's political and social fabric.

Facing widespread rebellion and loss of support, Díaz was forced to resign in May 1911 after Madero's forces, along with those led by Emiliano Zapata in the south and Pancho Villa in the north, gained momentum. Díaz went into exile in Paris, where he lived until his death in 1915 (aged 84). Despite the revolution that overthrew him, his influence on Mexico remained strong. The modernization programs he initiated had lasting effects on the country's infrastructure and economy, but the social inequalities his policies fostered became the central issues that the revolutionaries sought to address.

Porfirio Díaz remains a deeply controversial figure in Mexican history. For some, he's the leader who brought stability and progress to a fractured nation. For others, he's the autocrat whose oppressive regime deepened the inequality that led to a bloody revolution. In either case, Díaz's legacy is inextricably tied to the causes and consequences of the Mexican Revolution, which sought to dismantle the political and economic system he had created.

FRANCISCO MADERO

Fig 2

Francisco Madero's role in the Mexican Revolution is crucial, as his opposition to the long-standing dictatorship of Porfirio Díaz catalyzed the movement for change. Born into a wealthy family in 1873, Madero was educated abroad, where he developed progressive ideas about democracy, political reform, and social justice. studied business at the HEC

Paris (the Paris School of Advanced Business Studies). An advocate for social justice and democracy, Madero wrote and published a book in 1908 titled *The Presidential Succession in 1910*. Upon returning to Mexico, he became disillusioned with the Díaz regime, which had consolidated power through repression and election rigging.

In 1910, Madero published "La Sucesión Presidencial en 1910", a manifesto that called for free elections and democratic reform. He quickly became the figurehead of the anti-Díaz movement. After Díaz manipulated the 1910 elections to retain power, Madero called for an armed revolt, issuing the Plan de San Luis Potosí. This document called for the Mexican people to rise against Díaz on November 20, 1910, a date that marks the beginning of the Mexican Revolution.

The revolution spread quickly, with key leaders like Pancho Villa and Emiliano Zapata joining the cause. Madero's forces grew, and by May 1911, Díaz resigned and fled into exile, marking a significant victory for the revolutionaries. Madero assumed the presidency later that year, symbolizing a new era of democratic ideals.

However, Madero's presidency was fraught with challenges. His moderate reforms alienated both the revolutionary radicals and the old elite. In 1913, a military coup led by Victoriano Huerta, with the backing of U.S. interests, overthrew Madero. Madero was arrested and assassinated on February 22, 1913 (aged 39), cutting short his dream of a democratic Mexico.

Although his presidency was brief, Madero's vision and actions had an enduring impact. His opposition to Díaz laid the foundation for the revolution that would eventually reshape Mexico, and his assassination made him a martyr for democracy.

EMILIANO ZAPATA

Fig 3

Emiliano Zapata is one of the most iconic figures of the Mexican Revolution, remembered for his unwavering dedication to agrarian reform and the rights of the rural poor. Born in Anenecuilco, Morelos, in 1879,

Emiliano Zapata Salazar grew up in a village where the struggle for land was a daily reality. From an early age, he witnessed the exploitation of peasants by wealthy landowners who expanded their haciendas at the expense of communal lands. This deep-rooted injustice would shape Zapata's entire revolutionary vision.

Zapata became a leader of his community in the early 1900s, long before the revolution began. He gained a reputation as a fierce advocate for the rights of the indigenous and peasant populations, using both legal and extralegal means to protect their lands. By 1910, when Francisco Madero called for an uprising against the dictatorship of Porfirio Díaz, Zapata was already leading armed groups in southern Mexico, primarily focused on land reform.

Zapata's Plan de Ayala, issued in 1911, outlined his revolutionary ideals and called for the immediate return of stolen lands to peasants. The plan denounced Madero, who had assumed the presidency after Díaz's fall but failed to deliver on promises of agrarian reform. Zapata's cry of "Tierra y Libertad" (Land and Liberty) became the rallying call for his movement, and it drew thousands of peasants into his army, known as the Zapatistas.

Unlike many of the other revolutionary leaders, such as Pancho Villa in the north or Venustiano Carranza in the central regions, Zapata's focus remained singular: land reform for the rural poor. He fought not for personal power but for the redistribution of land and the dismantling of the hacienda system. His forces gained control over large swathes of territory in Morelos and neighboring states, where they implemented agrarian policies that prefigured the reforms that would later be adopted by the Mexican government.

Zapata's dedication to his cause often put him at odds with other revolutionary leaders. He refused to compromise on the issue of land reform, even as alliances shifted throughout the revolution. Zapata distrusted the central government, whether under Francisco Madero, Victoriano Huerta, or Venustiano Carranza, believing that true reform could only come from the grassroots. Yet, he never sought to hold a political office.

Zapata's reputation as a man of integrity and principle made him both a beloved leader among the peasants and a dangerous enemy to the ruling elites. His refusal to align with the centralizing forces of the revolution eventually led to his assassination in 1919 (aged 39). Lured into an ambush by one of Carranza's officers under the pretense of a meeting, Zapata was gunned down at the Hacienda de San Juan Chinameca. His death marked the end of the most ardent advocate for immediate land reform, but his ideals did not die with him.

Zapata became a symbol of resistance and martyrdom, and his vision of land reform continued to inspire agrarian movements long after his death. The Zapatista cry of "Tierra y Libertad" lived on, influencing not only Mexican policy but also broader global movements for indigenous and peasant rights. In the years following the revolution, some of Zapata's ideals were incorporated into the Mexican Constitution of 1917, although the full realization of his vision would take decades to materialize.

Emiliano Zapata remains a national hero in Mexico, his legacy representing the enduring struggle for social justice, equality, and dignity for the rural poor. Even today, he is celebrated as a symbol of the fight against oppression and for the fundamental right to land.

PANCHO VILLA

Fig 4

PANCHO VILLA, BORN JOSÉ DOROTEO ARANGO IN 1878, rose to prominence as one of the most charismatic and influential leaders of the Mexican Revolution. He commanded the formidable División del Norte and became a symbol of rebellion, particularly in northern

Mexico. Villa's revolutionary career was defined by his daring raids, military prowess, and fierce opposition to the oppressive regimes that ruled Mexico.

Villa's early life was marked by hardship. Born into a poor family in Durango, he grew up at one of the largest haciendas in the state, *Rancho de la Coyotada*. He became involved in a life of banditry at sixteen after killing a man who assaulted his sister. This period of lawlessness gave Villa an edge as a fearless fighter, and it was during these years that he developed the leadership skills and tenacity that would later serve him during the revolution. When Francisco Madero called for an uprising against Porfirio Díaz in 1910, Villa saw an opportunity to channel his efforts into a larger cause— the fight for justice and freedom.

Villa quickly became a key player in the revolution. Under Madero's leadership, he began to organize an army of revolutionaries in the north, composed mainly of ranchers, cowboys, and peasants who were dissatisfied with the inequalities perpetuated by Díaz's regime. Villa's army, known as the División del Norte, gained a reputation for its speed, mobility, and ferocity. Villa's knowledge of the land, support from the people, and use of both traditional military tactics and guerilla warfare allowed him to be a successful and brilliant military leader. He led successful campaigns, capturing key cities and territories that ultimately forced Díaz to resign in 1911.

Unlike other revolutionary leaders, such as Emiliano Zapata, Villa's focus was less on agrarian reform and more on the political changes necessary to rid Mexico of its dictatorial regimes. However, he still advocated for social justice and the redistribution of land to the poor.

Villa's forces were responsible for several major victories, including the famous Battle of Zacatecas in 1914, a decisive moment that helped secure the revolutionary forces' control of northern Mexico.

Despite his military success, Villa's relationship with other revolutionary leaders was complex. After Victoriano Huerta seized power and betrayed Madero, Villa joined forces with Venustiano Carranza to overthrow Huerta's government. However, once Huerta was defeated, Villa and Carranza clashed over the direction of the new government. Carranza's more conservative vision for Mexico conflicted with Villa's revolutionary ideals, leading to a split in the revolutionary movement.

By 1915, Villa's forces began to suffer setbacks, especially after a crushing defeat at the Battle of Celaya at the hands of Álvaro Obregón. With Carranza gaining political control, Villa's power diminished, and he eventually retreated into the northern mountains of Chihuahua, where he continued to wage a guerrilla campaign against the government. His bold raid on Columbus, New Mexico, in 1916 brought him international attention and led the U.S. to send a military expedition into Mexico to capture him, although they were ultimately unsuccessful.

Villa's revolutionary career officially ended in 1920, when he accepted a peace agreement from the Mexican government and retired to a ranch in Canutillo. However, his legacy remained a thorn in the side of the post-revolutionary government. Seen as a potential threat, Villa was assassinated on July 20, 1923 (aged 45), while traveling in his car in the town of Parral, Chihuahua. His death marked the end of one of Mexico's most famous and controversial revolutionaries.

Pancho Villa remains an enduring figure in Mexican history, remembered for his larger-than-life persona and his crucial role in the Mexican Revolution. Though his tactics were often brutal, and his politics complex, he is celebrated as a champion of the poor and an unrelenting fighter against injustice. Villa's leadership in the revolution cemented his place as one of the key figures in the movement that reshaped Mexico in the early twentieth century.

VICTORIANO HUERTA

Fig 5

Victoriano Huerta is one of the most infamous figures of the Mexican Revolution, remembered for betraying the revolutionary cause and installing himself as a dictator. Born in Colotlán, Jalisco, in 1845, Huerta was a career military man who had served under Porfirio Díaz and earned a reputation for his ruthless efficiency. He initially aligned with Francisco Madero after Díaz's ouster, but it wasn't long before Huerta's ambitions led him to turn against the revolutionary government.

In 1911, Madero had ascended to the presidency following Díaz's resignation, but his moderate reforms alienated many factions. Among those who grew disillusioned was Huerta, who saw an opportunity to seize power. He allied himself with conservative forces, including remnants of the old Díaz regime and foreign business interests who were frustrated by Madero's inability to maintain order.

The pivotal moment came in February 1913, during what is known as La Decena Trágica (The Ten Tragic Days), a violent ten-day coup in Mexico City. Huerta, who was Madero's top general at the time, turned against him and joined forces with Félix Díaz (Porfirio Díaz's nephew) and the U.S. ambassador, Henry Lane Wilson, in a plot to overthrow the president. Madero was arrested, and shortly afterward, both Madero and his vice president, José María Pino Suárez, were assassinated. Huerta declared himself president, plunging Mexico into further turmoil.

Huerta's rule was marked by repression, corruption, and a return to the authoritarianism of the Porfiriato era. His military background meant that he governed with an iron fist, crushing dissent and attempting to consolidate power through force. However, his regime faced immediate resistance from various revolutionary leaders, including Venustiano Carranza, Pancho Villa, and Emiliano Zapata, who all rallied against him.

Internationally, Huerta's government was isolated. Although some foreign powers initially supported him, the United States, under President Woodrow Wilson, refused to recognize his regime and even supported the revolutionaries fighting against him. By 1914, Huerta's military was losing ground to the revolutionary forces. The final blow came when U.S. Marines occupied Veracruz, cutting off Huerta's ability to receive arms shipments from abroad.

With his army collapsing and his political support eroding, Huerta resigned the presidency in July 1914 and fled to exile. He initially sought asylum in Europe before attempting to return to Mexico via the United States. However, Huerta was arrested by U.S. authorities in El Paso, Texas, and imprisoned for plotting to reenter Mexican politics. He died in prison in 1916 (aged 65), leaving behind a legacy as one of the most reviled figures of the Mexican Revolution.

Victoriano Huerta is remembered as a symbol of betrayal and authoritarianism. His brief but brutal dictatorship galvanized the revolutionary movement, uniting factions that had previously been divided. His downfall paved the way for the next phase of the revolution, where revolutionary leaders like Carranza, Villa, and Zapata would continue their fight to reshape Mexico's political and social landscape.

VENUSTIANO CARRANZA

Fig 6

Venustiano Carranza was a key figure in the Mexican Revolution and the architect of Mexico's Constitution of 1917, which laid the foundation for the modern Mexican state. He's also credited for maintaining Mexico's neutrality in WWI. Born into a wealthy landowning family in Coahuila in 1859, Carranza's background initially placed him in the conservative elite. However, he was drawn to the cause of reform and opposed the long-standing dictatorship of Porfirio Díaz.

Carranza's rise to prominence began during the early days of the revolution. After Francisco Madero ousted Díaz, Carranza was appointed governor of Coahuila. He aligned himself with Madero's vision of a democratic Mexico but became a staunch opponent of Victoriano Huerta after Huerta's betrayal and the assassination of Madero in 1913. Carranza formed the Constitutionalist Army, rallying revolutionary forces against Huerta's dictatorship. His forces, including key allies such as Álvaro Obregón and Pancho Villa, played a pivotal role in Huerta's defeat in 1914.

Once Huerta was overthrown, Carranza declared himself the First Chief of the Constitutional Army, effectively becoming the head of the revolutionary government. However, his consolidation of power was not without conflict. Carranza's vision of a constitutional republic clashed with the more radical social reforms demanded by Emiliano Zapata and Villa. Tensions escalated into civil war, with Carranza emerging victorious after a series of military campaigns, largely due to the strategic prowess of Obregón.

In 1917, Carranza's leadership culminated in the drafting of the Mexican Constitution, a groundbreaking document that introduced a range of progressive reforms, including labor rights, land redistribution, and the separation of church and state. The Constitution of 1917 is still in effect today and is considered one of Carranza's greatest legacies. His moderate approach, however, left many revolutionaries dissatisfied, particularly those like Zapata, who sought more immediate and radical land reforms.

Carranza became president in 1917 and focused on stabilizing the country after years of revolutionary upheaval. His government, while advancing reforms, also faced internal divisions and the lingering effects of the revolution. Carranza's presidency was marked by efforts to modernize Mexico, although his policies often favored the elites and urban middle class over the rural poor.

By 1920, Carranza's grip on power began to weaken, particularly as Obregón and other revolutionary leaders turned against him. In an attempt to handpick a successor, Carranza alienated many of his former allies. A rebellion led by Obregón forced Carranza to flee Mexico City. In May 1920, while attempting to escape to Veracruz, Carranza was assassinated at sixty years old by forces loyal to Obregón.

Venustiano Carranza's legacy is complex. He is remembered as the leader who brought an end to Huerta's dictatorship and restored constitutional order to Mexico. His greatest achievement, the Constitution of 1917, shaped the political and social framework of modern Mexico. However, his inability to reconcile the competing demands of the various revolutionary factions left the country deeply divided. Carranza's death marked the end of his brand of constitutionalism, but his influence on the future of Mexican governance remains undeniable.

Enter into a World of Warfare History

Explore Military History And Warfare Stories From The 20th Century

Get your free copy of WW2: Spies, Snipers, and Tales of the World at War and dive into the stories that changed the world.

Send me my free Ebook

Go to wrinnmilitaryhistory.com and get your free book **WW2: Spies, Snipers and Tales of the World at War**. I'll also add you to my military history readers group where I occasionally send out emails with details on new releases and special offers.

BIBLIOGRAPHY

Blum, Howard. *Dark Invasion: 1915 – Germany's Secret War*. Harper, 2014.

Brunk, Samuel. *Emiliano Zapata: Revolution and Betrayal in Mexico*. Albuquerque: University of New Mexico Press, 1995.

Cumberland, Charles C. *Mexican Revolution: The Constitutional Years*. Austin: University of Texas Press, 1972.

Katz, Friedrich. *The Life and Times of Pancho Villa*. Stanford: Stanford University Press, 1998.

Knight, Alan. *The Mexican Revolution*. 2 vols. Cambridge: Cambridge University Press, 1986.

McLynn, Frank. *Villa and Zapata: A History of the Mexican Revolution*. New York: Basic Books, 2000.

Meyer, Jean. *The Cristero Rebellion: The Mexican People between Church and State, 1926–1929*. Cambridge: Cambridge University Press, 1976.

Time. "MEXICO: The Man Who Killed Villa." *TIME*, June 4, 1951. https://time.com/archive/6795539/mexico-the-man-who-killed-villa/.

Wikipedia contributors. "President of Mexico." *Wikipedia*. Last modified October 10, 2024. https://en.wikipedia.org/wiki/President_of_Mexico.

Womack, John. *Zapata and the Mexican Revolution*. New York: Vintage Books, 1969.

Image Credits:

Got it! Here's how you can include the attribution for General Victoriano Huerta along with the others. Since it's under a CC0 license, you can still credit it in a similar manner.

Image Credits

Fig. 1 Porfirio Díaz, 1910, by A Escobar C, from the digital archive "Mexico's Hundred Years of Independence Festivity," public domain via Wikimedia Commons.

Fig. 2 Portrait of Francisco I. Madero, 1914, from the United States Library of Congress's Prints and Photographs division (Digital ID: ggbain.01887), public domain.

Fig. 3 Emiliano Zapata, 1914, by Agustín Casasola, public domain via Wikimedia Commons.

Fig. 4 Pandcho Villa bandolier.jpg By Bain News Service, Publisher. Public domain via Wikimedia Commons

Fig. 5 General Victoriano Huerta, 1912, by PorVicAn, CC0 via Wikimedia Commons.

Fig. 6 Portrait of President Venustiano Carranza, cropped and reuploaded by Emiya1980, originally by Harris & Ewing, from The World's Work, 1915, public domain via Wikimedia Commons.

during this conflicted time, along with letters and journal entries from decades ago, this memoir is a testament to the sacrifice that these brave men and women made fighting on foreign soil.

Recounting the tragedies of war and the chaos of combat as an infantry soldier, in the words of the author: "We lived, and fought as a unit, covering each other's backs. Most came home to tell their own stories, many didn't."

If you like gripping, authentic accounts of life and combat during the Vietnam War, then you won't want to miss Mongoose Bravo: Vietnam: A Time of Reflection Over Events So Long Ago.

World War II Pacific: Battles and Campaigns from Guadalcanal to Okinawa 1942-1945

"A brisk and compelling game changer for the historiography of the Pacific Theater in World War II." – Reviewer

An enlightening glimpse into nine battles and campaigns during the Pacific War Allied offensive.

Each of these momentous operations were fascinating feats of strategy, planning, and bravery, handing the Allies what would eventually become a victory over the Pacific Theater and an end to Imperialist Japanese expansion.

Operation Watchtower, a riveting exploration of the spark that set off the Allied offensive in the Pacific islands, detailing the grueling struggle for the island of Guadalcanal and its vital strategic position.

Operation Galvanic, an incredible account of the battle for the Tarawa Atoll and base that would give them a steppingstone into the heart of Japanese-controlled waters.

Operation Backhander, a gripping retelling of the war for Cape Gloucester, New Guinea, and the Bismarck Sea.

Battle for Saipan, Marines stormed the beaches with a goal of gaining a crucial air base from which the US could launch its new long-range B-29 bombers directly at Japan's home islands.

Invasion of Tinian, is the incredible account of the assault on Tinian. Located just under six miles southwest of Saipan. This was the first use of napalm and the "shore to shore" concept.

Recapture of Guam, a gripping narrative about the liberation of the Japanese-held island of Guam, captured by the Japanese in 1941 during one of the first Pacific campaigns of the War.

Operation Stalemate, Marines landed on the island of Peleliu, one of the Palau Islands in the Pacific, as part of a larger operation to provide support for General MacArthur, who was preparing to invade the Philippines.

Operation Detachment, the battle of Iwo Jima was a major offensive in World War II. The Marine invasion was tasked with the mission of capturing airfields on the island for use by P-51 fighters.

Operation Iceberg, the invasion and ultimate victory on Okinawa was the largest amphibious assault in the Pacific Theater. It was also one of the bloodiest battles in the Pacific, lasting ninety-eight days.

This gripping narrative sheds light on these often-overlooked facets of WWII, providing students, history fans, and World War II buffs alike with a captivating breakdown of the history and combat that defined the ultimate victory of US forces in the Pacific.

Broken Wings: WWI Fighter Ace's Story of Escape and Survival

"A masterfully told story of triumph and redemption in a powerfully drawn survival epic." – Reviewer

Hero WWI Fighter Pilot Shot Down and Captured.

With an engaging and authentic retelling of his experiences as an escaped prisoner of war, this gripping account details the life and struggles of a captured pilot in 1917 war-torn Europe.

Lieutenant John Ryan couldn't wait to see action in WWI. He joined up with the British colors out of Canada. As one of several American pilots in the Royal Flying Corps before the US joined the war, he earned his wings and became an Ace through fierce air battles over the skies of Germany.

www.ingramcontent.com/pod-product-compliance
Lightning Source LLC
Chambersburg PA
CBHW031433130726
47989CB00003B/1119